FUN JOKES

for kids

More Than
500
SQUEAKY-CLEAN,
Super Silly,
Laugh-It-Up
Jokes for Kids Ages 8–12

© 2014 by Barbour Publishing, Inc.

ISBN 978-1-62416-686-0

eBook Editions:
Adobe Digital Edition (.epub) 978-1-62836-371-5
Kindle and MobiPocket Edition (.prc) 978-1-62836-372-2

All scripture quotations are taken from the King James Version of the Bible.

Published by Barbour Publishing, Inc., P.O. Box 719, Uhrichsville, Ohio 44683, www.barbourbooks.com

Our mission is to publish and distribute inspirational products offering exceptional value and biblical encouragement to the masses.

Member of the
Evangelical Christian
Publishers Association

Printed in the United States of America.
Offset Paper Manufacturers, Dallas, PA 18612; January 2014;
D10004301

CONTENTS

⊙ ∘ ⊙ ∘ ⊙ ∘ ⊙

INTRODUCTION

⊙ • ⊙ • ⊙ • ⊙

Kids love to laugh—and here's a fantastic collection of more than 500 jokes and funny stories especially for the younger set!

Fun Jokes for Kids contains plenty of squeaky-clean, super silly, laugh-it-up jokes that you can tell your mom or dad. . . grandma. . .pastor. . .even your dog. (Just don't expect him to laugh out loud.)

Jokes are arranged by topic—from Aardvarks to Zebras, and everything in between—and each section includes an inspirational introduction that adds just a touch of scripture! What could be better than that?

All righty, then. . .turn the page for *Fun Jokes for Kids!*

SECTION 1

BUGS, BIRDS, AND BEASTS

*And God made the beast of the earth
after his kind, and cattle after their kind,
and every thing that creepeth upon
the earth after his kind: and God
saw that it was good.*
GENESIS 1:25

◉ ◦ ◉ ◦ ◉ ◦ ◉

Sure, we all love dogs. Most of us like cats—
kittens at least. Horses are pretty cool. But
worms? Ticks? Bats? Aardvarks? Hey, God
made 'em and called 'em "good." And they lend
themselves to a little joke now and then!

AARDVARKS AND ANTEATERS

What animal looks a lot like an aardvark?

Another aardvark.

Why are anteaters so healthy?

Because they are high on ant-i-bodies!

ALLIGATORS

What's green and white and green and white and green and white?

An alligator somersaulting downhill.

If an instigator instigates, does an alligator alligate?

ANTS

Marie: "I think the ant is just the coolest animal! It works all day—and do you know how much it can get accomplished?"

Matt: "Yeah, a lot until somebody steps on it."

When do ants travel fastest?

When they get on the anterstate highway.

What do you call an elderly ant?

An ant-ique.

Nell: "Is it true that ants are the hardest-working creatures?"

Science teacher: "That's what a lot of scientists believe."

Nell: "Then why are they always attending picnics?"

How do you keep ants from digging mounds all over your yard?

Take away their shovels.

Why do hikers wear boots with ridged soles?

> *So ants will have an even chance.*

APES

What do you call a flying ape?

> *A hot-air baboon.*

BATS

What kind of animal is always found at baseball games?

> *The bat.*

BEARS

Tim: "I've heard bears won't chase you at night if you carry a flashlight."

Kim: "Depends on how fast you carry it."

What's large, white, fierce, eats salmon, and lives in the Sahara Desert?

A polar bear that got lost.

Why does a bear sleep three months out of the year?

No one is brave enough to wake it up.

"Someone's been eating my soup!" shouted Papa Bear.

"Someone's been eating my soup!" shouted Mama Bear.

"Hooray!" shouted Baby Bear. "Does that mean we can have ice cream for supper?"

Where do bears like to stay when they go on vacation?

At cave-inns.

Where do bears get their news?

From cub reporters.

"My feet are sore," one bear said to another. "I'm going to the mall to buy tennis shoes."

"What for?" asked his friend. "You're still going to have bear feet."

What's black and white, black and white, black and white?

A panda bear rolling down the mountain.

Brad: "Why do bears paint their faces yellow?"

Lad: "Don't know."

Brad: "So they can hide in banana trees."

Lad: "Impossible. I've never seen a bear in a banana tree."

Brad: "That's because they've painted their faces yellow."

Why does a bear hibernate for three months in cold weather?

We're all afraid to wake it up!

Two guys were hiking in the forest when they suddenly came across a big grizzly bear. The one guy took off his hiking boots and put on some running shoes. His friend said to him, "You're crazy! Don't you know how fast grizzlies are? You'll never be able to outrun it!

"Outrun it?" said his friend. "I only have to out run you!"

What is a polar bear's favorite place to vacation?

Brrr-muda.

What do you call a grizzly bear with no teeth?

A gummy bear.

Where do polar bears vote?

The North Poll.

BEAVERS

How does a beaver know which tree to cut down?

Whichever one he chews.

BEES

Why won't you find much honey grown in Maryland?

> *There's only one B in Baltimore.*

"What's in style this season?" an insect asked a tailor.

> *"Yellow jackets."*

What do bees like to chew?

> *Buzzlegum.*

What's the difference between a bee and a fly?

You can't zip a bee.

Sissy: "Have you heard they're now making a special kind of ground meat out of bumblebees?"
　Missy: "Yuk! What do they call that?"
　Sissy: "Humburger."

Maria: "My school class has adopted a talking bird!"
　Patsy: "That's nothing. My class has a spelling bee."

BEETLES

"It's New Year's Day," said one beetle to another. "Have you made any resolutions?"

"Yeah," said the other. "I'm gonna turn over a new leaf."

BIRDS IN GENERAL

How high is the sky?

High enough that birds don't have to worry about bumping their heads.

What is a bird's favorite food?

Chocolate chirp cookies.

"My parakeet has proposed marriage," said Roger.

"Who does it want to marry?" asked Drew.

"Its childhood tweetheart."

Teacher: "What kinds of birds are commonly found in jungles?"

Student: "Hot, sweaty birds."

Why were the birds punished?

For using fowl language.

Why did the songbird go to the doctor?

To be tweeted.

What kind of birds live in Central America?

Birds with suntans.

What birds spend time on their knees?

Birds of prey.

"That's the biggest bird I've ever seen!"

"It's only a swallow."

"Swallow? That's more like a gulp!"

BUFFALOS

What did the mother buffalo say to her boy as he was leaving?

"Bison."

CATERPILLARS

One caterpillar to another, as they watch a butterfly: "You'll never get me up in one of those things."

CATS

Why couldn't the cat slip through the eye of a needle?

Someone tied a knot in its tail.

What do you call the grandfather of a kitten?

A grandpaw.

How did the kitten get to the top of the tree?

It stood on an acorn and waited for it to grow.

What kind of cars do kittens drive?

Catillacs.

How did the cat succeed in winning a starring role in a movie?

With purr-sistence.

"Jack, put out the cat," Mother instructed as the family got ready for bed.

"I can't, Mom."

"Why not?"

"Because it hasn't come in all day." When you call a dog, they usually come to you. When you call a cat, they take a message.

"Jenny!" screamed her mother, "why are you feeding birdseed to the cat?"

"I have to," Jenny replied. "That's where my canary is."

Why was the cat afraid of the tree?

Because of its bark.

"What is your cat's favorite food?" asked David.

"Mice cream," said Micah.

"Have you got any kittens going cheap?" asked a customer in a pet shop.

"No, sir," replied the owner. "All our kittens go, 'Meow.'"

CATTLE

Why did the cow jump over the moon?

It forgot where it left its rocket ship.

What do you call a bull taking a nap?

A bulldozer.

Why doesn't the cow wear a bell?

Two horns are enough warning.

How can you guarantee milk won't go sour?

Don't milk the cow.

Why did the cow cross the road?

To see what was on the udder side.

What animal says "oom"?

A backward cow.

What do you call a cow eating grass in your yard?

A lawn moo-er.

Why did the cow enroll in drama class?

To become a moo-vie star.

"If a cow's head is pointed west, in which direction is its tail pointed?" Wade asked.
   "East," said Wyatt.
   "No," said Wade. "It's pointed down."

How do you count a herd of cows?

With a cowculator.

Where do cows go on dates?

To the moo-vie.

What do you hear when cows start singing?

Moo-sic.

CHICKENS

Why did the chicken cross the playground?

To get to the other slide.

What chicken was a famous Antarctic explorer?

Admiral Bird.

Who was the least favorite president of chickens?

Herbert Hoover. He promised, "A chicken in every pot."

Why did the chicken cross the road?

To avoid Colonel Sanders.

Why did the chewing gum cross the road?

It was stuck to the bottom of the chicken's shoe.

What's the best way to move a chicken?

Pullet.

What do chickens have to be thankful for on Thanksgiving Day?

The fact that they're not turkeys.

How do young chicks escape from their eggs?

Through the eggs-its.

What disease do chickens dread the most?

People pox.

What did the Navy get when it crossed a chicken with a case of dynamite?

A mine layer.

How do you catch a chicken?

Hide in the yard and act like a corn kernel.

Who is the favorite actor of chickens?

Gregory Peck.

Why did the chicken go to New York City?

> *To visit the Henpire State Building.*

What is the favorite musical of chickens?

> *Fiddler on the Roost.*

Why did the rooster cluck at midnight?

> *His cluck was fast.*

Why did the rock band hire a chicken?

> *They needed the drumsticks.*

Why was the chicken sitting on the eggplant?

> *She was nearsighted.*

Candice: "I'm afraid to buy eggs at the supermarket because when I break them open at home I might discover they have little chicks inside them."

Lennie: "Then why don't you buy goose eggs?"

Two hens were pecking in the yard when suddenly a softball came sailing over the fence, landing a few feet away from them. One hen said to another, "Will you just look at the ones they're turning out next door!"

Chicken to turkey: "Only Thanksgiving and Christmas? You're lucky; with us, it's any Sunday."

COYOTES

Why do coyotes call at night?

The rates are cheaper.

DOGS

"Mom, the dog bit sister's hand again!"

"Uh-oh. We'd better take a look. We may need to put something on it."

"Nah, I think the dog prefers her hand plain."

Why did the dog refuse to wear its wristwatch?

Because the watch had ticks.

A salesman entered a yard and saw two little girls playing with a dog.

"Does your dog bite?" he asked the children.

"Oh no, sir. Our dog has never bitten anyone."

The salesman then walked up the steps to ring the doorbell for the parents. Suddenly, the dog jumped on the porch and bit him fiercely on the leg.

"Hey, you said your dog doesn't bite!" the salesman yelled at the girls.

"Our dog doesn't. That's somebody else's dog."

What do you call a puppy who loves anchovies and garlic?

A dog whose bark is a thousand times worse than his bite.

Mickie: "My bulldog came away from the bird show with first prize."

Vickie: "How could a dog do that?"

Mickie: "He ate the winning parrot."

What did Natasha do when she found her pet dog eating her dictionary?

She took the words right out of his mouth.

"Tracie's dog looks just like a member of her family," said Stacie.

"Which one?" asked Macie.

Where's the best place to park dogs?

In a barking lot.

Maria: "I can always tell when my dog is happy."

Michael: "Does he wag his tail?"

Maria: "No, but he stops biting me."

Blake: "My dog's the smartest in town. He can say his own name in perfect English."

Alice: "What's his name?"

Blake: "Ruff."

A pet shop owner was trying to talk Mrs. McLellan into buying a dog for her children. "Oh, they'll love this little rascal!" said the clerk. "He's full of fun and he eats anything. He especially likes children."

Sue: "Dogs are terrible dancers."

Allen: "How do you know that?"

Sue: "They have two left feet."

What was the dog doing in the mud puddle?

Making mutt pies.

Bart: "Our house was robbed last night while we were out."

Bret: "But I thought Butch was a great watchdog."

Bart: "Apparently he watched them take everything in sight."

How do you make a puppy disappear?

Use Spot remover.

Police were investigating a break-in.

"Didn't you hear any strange noises next door last evening?" they asked one neighbor.

"We couldn't hear anything. Their dog was barking too loud."

Rachel: "Did you know dogs eat more than elephants?"

Penny: "No way! How can they do that?"

Rachel: "There are thousands of times more dogs in the world than there are elephants.

Why do firemen have dogs for mascots?

To help them locate the fire hydrants.

Myra: "Our dog must be older than we thought."

Luke: "What makes you think so?"

Myra: "She's started bringing in yesterday's newspaper."

What do you call a nature film about dogs?

A dog-umentary.

At what point in history were dogs happiest?

During the Bone Age.

"If you were being chased by two German shepherds," posed Erin, "what steps would you take?"

"Long ones," said Bart.

"Does your dog Dolly have fleas?" asked Brianne.

"No—but she just had puppies!" said Erica.

A woman frantically dialed 911. "You've got to help me," she said. "I've lost my dog!"

"Sorry, ma'am," said the dispatcher, "but we don't handle missing animals."

"You don't understand. This is no ordinary dog. He can talk."

"Well, you better hang up. He might be trying to call in."

"We had to buy our dog a longer leash," Zan said.

"Why?" asked Van.

"Dad kept stepping on his tail."

"What do you think of my police dog?"

"Dog? That animal says 'meow'!"

"Yes. He's working undercover at the moment."

What sign did the bulldog put in front of its doghouse?

Beware of Resident

"What's your dog's name?"

"Ginger, when she's not biting people."

"What's her name when she *is* biting people?"

"Ginger Snaps."

What do you get when you cross a Dalmatian with a fountain pen?

Ink spots.

The Johnsons invited their new neighbors the Andersons for dinner. Everyone was having a great time, enjoying the food and conversation. Mr. Anderson was curious, though, to observe that the Johnsons' dog sat right beside him on the floor and stared at him the whole evening.

"This is a very nice dog you have," Mr. Anderson said. "But I wonder why he keeps looking at me like that."

"Probably," the Johnsons' little boy suggested, "it's because you're eating off of his plate."

A movie screenwriter waited eagerly for word on whether her latest work had been accepted by any of the film companies. She hounded her agent every day. Finally, the agent phoned her to report.

"Good news," the agent said. "Warner Brothers loved your script and literally ate it up."

"That's wonderful!" beamed the screenwriter. "So when will they be making the movie?"

"Well, there's one small problem. Warner Brothers is my dog. . . ."

In a small town the veterinarian, who was also the chief of police, was awakened by the telephone.

"Please hurry!" said the woman's voice on the other end of the line.

"Do you need the police or a vet?" he asked.

"Both," the woman replied. "I'm not able to get my dog's mouth open, and there's a burglar's leg in it."

What bone will a dog never eat?

A trombone.

What would you get if you crossed a hunting dog and a telephone?

A golden receiver.

How does a dog turn off the DVR?

He presses the paws button.

What did the dog get when he multiplied 413 by 782?

The wrong answer.

What should you do if you find a five-hundred-pound dog wearing your favorite tie?

> Go see a doctor. You have been seeing too many five-hundred-pound dogs lately.

A hound dog and a Dalmatian were sitting in an Internet café. The Dalmatian said to the hound, "Hey, check out my website!"

The hound asked for the address and the Dalmatian responded, "www.dalmatian.dot-dot-dot-dot-dot-dot-dot-dot."

What do you call a dog with a receding hairline?

> Bald Spot!

Ducks

What goes "quick-quick"?

A duck with the hiccups.

What do you call a mallard's last will and testament?

A legal duckument.

Where do ducks prefer to go on vacation?

The Duck-otas.

EGRETS

Why does the egret stand on one leg?

Because if it lifts the other leg, it falls.

ELEPHANTS

How do you stop an elephant from chasing you?

With elephant repellent.

Two children were at the zoo. "Elephants sure are fat animals," commented one.

"Yeah. I guess my mom was right when she said peanuts are fattening."

William: "I can stop a charging elephant with one hand."

Pete: "I don't believe an elephant with one hand would be charging."

How does an elephant get down a chimney?

It volunteers as one of Santa's helpers and hides in the toy sack.

How do you trap an elephant?

Take a big net, hide in the jungle, and sound like a peanut.

What's huge, gray, has a trunk, and goes up and down?

An elephant on an elevator.

What wears beautiful slippers and weighs several tons?

Cinderelephant.

What do you get when you cross an elephant with an overloaded computer?

A crash through the jungle.

If an elephant falls into a cup of coffee, what's the result?

Death by drowning. Elephants don't swim well in coffee.

What do you get when you cross an elephant with peanut butter?

An elephant that sticks to the roof of your mouth.

What kind of vegetable do you find under elephants' feet?

Squash.

What did the elephants wear at the swimming pool?

Trunks.

Why are elephants so wrinkled?

They're too difficult to iron.

How do elephants communicate?

With elephones.

How do you make an elephant float?

Start with your favorite ice cream, pour cola over it, and add elephant.

Why is a snail small and smooth?

> *Because if it were huge and wrinkled, it would be an elephant.*

What's big and gray and has a trunk and goes "zrrrrrrrrrrrr"?

> *An outboard elephant.*

What's the difference between Superman and an elephant?

> *The elephant wears a big "E" on his chest.*

Why was the elephant wearing a purple T-shirt?

His other shirts were all at the cleaners.

How do you treat an elephant with seasickness?

Give it a lot of space.

What is as big as an elephant but doesn't weigh an ounce?

An elephant's shadow.

FIREFLIES

What are nature's busiest insects?

Fireflies. They're always on the glow.

Jim and Ward were camping out one summer evening, and mosquitoes were a terrible problem. About dark, a different type of insect made its presence known: fireflies, darting here and there throughout the forest.

"Wow! Look at those mosquitoes!" cried Jim.

"Oh, no!" Ward said. "I thought we could hide from them in the dark, but they're coming after us with flashlights!"

FiSH

"Jerry, I insist that you take your little brother fishing with you," Dad said sternly.

"But Dad, he—"

"No buts. He needs to learn how to fish, and you can teach him while I'm busy here in the shop."

"But Dad, he—"

"I told you, no buts. Now go."

"But there's no bait."

"What do you mean? I just bought you a box of crickets."

"Little brother has already eaten 'em all."

What's the most famous fish in the world?

The starfish.

"I keep my goldfish in a huge tank," said Mark.
"I keep mine in the bathtub," said Mitch.
"In the bathtub? What do you do with them when you need to take a bath?"
"I make them cover their eyes."

How do you catch a school of fish?

With a bookworm.

Blake: "We're not catching any fish. Why don't you tell them to start biting?"

Jake: "How can I communicate with a fish?"

Blake: "Drop them another line."

Kippie: "I caught a fish yesterday that weighed ten pounds!"

Mickie: "I don't believe it."

Kippie: "It's true. The picture alone weighed almost a pound."

In what country can fish survive out of water?

Finland.

What did the fish boat captain say to the card magician?

"Pick a cod, any cod."

What are the first things fish learn in school?

Their A-B-Seas.

Who are hammerhead sharks' best friends?

Nailhead sharks.

"You can't catch fish here," the game warden told Timmy. "You don't have a license."

"Well, I haven't had a bite all day," Timmy said. "I doubt I could catch fish here even if I did have a license."

Why do goldfish have to be kept inside?
Because they'll slip through the leash if you try to take them out for a walk.

What are tropical fishes' favorite foods?

Reef-fried beans.

Two boys were walking home from the creek with a nice string of fish. They'd had a great day fishing, but their prizes were starting to emit a strong, unpleasant odor.

"I sure wish there was some way we could keep 'em from smelling," said one boy.

"Well," said the other, "I reckon we could clamp their noses."

What do you call a fish with no eye?

A fsh.

FLEAS

What highways do dogs and cats hate most?

Fleaways.

Stephanie: "Did you know I used to own a flea circus?"

    Webster: "No. What happened to it?"

    Stephanie: "A stray dog came along one day and stole the show."

Two fleas hopped down the steps onto the sidewalk. One turned to the other and asked, "Should we walk, or take a dog?"

Why did the flea work overtime?

> *It was saving up to buy a dog.*

FOXES

What did one fox say to another?

> *"I'm tired of being hounded
> all the time."*

FROGS

What goes "CROAK! CROAK!" on
foggy nights?

> *A froghorn.*

"My pet frog can work math problems," bragged Buster.

"No way," said Bryce. "Show me."

Buster held his frog in his palm and asked it, "What's ten minus ten?"

And the frog said nothing.

The question on the biology test asked: "Name three kinds of frogs."

The student wrote: "Daddy frog, mama frog, baby frog."

What do you call a nine-foot-high stack of frogs?

A toadem pole.

What kind of shoes do frogs wear?

Open-toad slippers.

What's the best way to clear frogs off your car windows?

With the defrogger.

"Let's go see a movie," suggested one frog to another.

"Okay. I hope it has a hoppy ending."

How do frogs handle stress?

When something bugs them, they simply eat it.

What do you get when you cross a frog and a chair?

A toadstool.

What would you get if you crossed a baseball player with a frog?

> *An outfielder who catches flies. . .*
> *and then eats them.*

What animal has more lives than a cat?

> *A frog, because he croaks*
> *every night.*

What happens when a frog's car breaks down?

> *He gets toad away.*

GEESE

What should you do when someone throws a goose at you?

Duck.

GIRAFFES

What do you call a story told by a giraffe?

A tall tale.

Why does a giraffe have a long neck?

So it can't smell its feet.

Why do giraffes have such small appetites?

Because with them, a little goes a long way.

What is worse than a giraffe with a sore neck?

A centipede with athlete's foot.

Why did the giraffe graduate early?

He was head and shoulders above the rest.

GOATS

What kind of infants prefer goat milk?

Infant goats.

Why is it hard to talk to a ram?

He keeps butting in.

Why did the goat stick its head through the barbed wire fence?

To see what was on the other side.

Two goats wandered into the junkyard and had a field day. One of them spent a particularly long time bent over a spool of film. When he was finished, the other goat came over. "So, did you enjoy the film?"

The goat replied, "To tell you the truth, I liked the book better."

GRASSHOPPERS

What kind of surgery is done in grasshopper hospitals?

Hoperations.

HAMSTERS

Teacher: "If I give you four hamsters and your brother three hamsters, how many hamsters will you have altogether?"

Student: "Ten. We have three already."

What's the favorite city of hamsters?

Hamsterdam.

HAWKS

"Look at that speed!" said one hawk to another as the jet fighter plane zoomed over their heads.

"Hmph!" snorted the other. "You would fly fast, too, if your tail was on fire!"

HiPPOPOTAMUSES

What's huge and gray and goes around in circles?

*A hippopotamus in
a revolving door.*

79

What's the happiest animal in the wild?

The happypotamus.

How do you save a hippopotamus drowning in hot cocoa?

Throw it a marshmallow.

HORSES

Why do horses make such awkward dancers?

They have two left feet.

"How's your sick horse?" one rancher asked another.

"She's in stable condition."

"Grandpa, why is it that horses can stand up and walk so much sooner after they're born than humans can?" Neil asked.

"Well, it's partly because they have twice as many legs as humans do, I suppose."

Why did the rancher take the horse to the vet?

The horse had hay fever.

What kind of horse sees just as well with its tail as with its head?

A horse that's asleep.

Alicia: "Do you know what it means when you find a horseshoe?"

Pat: "Yes. It means some poor horse probably has a sore foot by now."

What did one horse say to the other when they ran out of hay?

"Now that's the last straw!"

A cowboy rides into town on Friday, stays three days and leaves on Friday. How does he do it?

His horse's name is Friday.

Which side of a horse usually has the most hair?

The outside.

HUMMINGBIRDS

Why do hummingbirds hum?

They've never learned the words.

How can you tell a guy hummingbird from a girl hummingbird?

By his mustache.

INSECTS IN GENERAL

"We have a real problem with biting insects around our yard," a customer told a pharmacist. "What can we do about it?"

"Stop biting them," said the pharmacist.

Ida: "What's orange and has green spots, eight legs, and one red eye?"

Erma: "I give up. What?"

Ida: "I don't know, but there's one crawling up your back."

KANGAROOS

Why do kangaroos paint themselves green?

So they can hide in a bowl of spinach.

Why did the kangaroo lose the basketball game?

He ran out of bounds.

What do you get when you cross an elephant with a kangaroo?

Big holes all over Australia.

Why does a mother kangaroo hope it doesn't rain?

> *She doesn't like it when the kids have to play inside.*

What kind of money do kangaroos use?

> *Pocket change.*

LADYBUGS

What kind of insect marries a ladybug?

> *A gentlemanbug.*

LEOPARDS

How does a leopard change its spots?

*When it's tired of one spot,
it just moves to another.*

LIONS

Nina: "I heard you just got back from Africa!
Did you hunt wild game?"
Stevie: "Yeah, lions."
Nina: "Did you have any luck?"
Stevie: "Yep. Didn't see a one."

Why can't you telephone the zoo?

The lion's busy.

LOBSTERS

Why do lobsters have a hard time sharing?

Because they're shellfish.

MICE

What do you call mouse shoes?

Squeakers.

How do mice keep their breath fresh all day long?

They rinse with mousewash.

Why did the mouse give up tap dancing?

It kept falling in the sink.

What's gray and has four legs and a trunk?

A mouse on vacation.

What do you do when a mouse squeaks?

Oil it.

A mother mouse and a baby mouse were walking along when all of a sudden, a cat attacked them. The mother mouse said, "Bark!" and the cat ran away.

"See?" said the mother mouse to her baby. "Now do you see why it's important to learn a foreign language?"

MONKEYS

How do you fix a broken chimp?

With a monkey wrench.

MOOSE

Why do moose have fur coats?

They don't like wearing cotton.

OCTOPi

What did the boy octopus say to the girl octopus?

> *"Can I hold your hand, hand, hand, hand, hand, hand, hand, hand?"*

First octopus: "What *do you* like least about being an octopus?"

Second octopus: "Washing my hands before dinner."

How does an octopus go into battle?

> *Fully armed.*

OPOSSUMS

Why did the chicken cross the road?

To show the opossum it could be done.

OSTRICHES

A band of pirates buried their treasure on the seashore. Afterward, they looked around for a marker but could find nothing except a few ostrich eggs. So they broke open the eggs, fried the yolks, and left the shells on top of the buried treasure.

The pirate captain announced to his crew, "Eggs mark the spot."

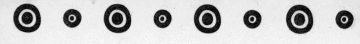

OTTERS

Why did the otter cross the road?

> *To get to the otter side.*

OWLS

Why do owls fly around at night?

> *It's faster than walking.*

"What kind of bird is the best protector?" asked the teacher.

> *"The knight owl," answered the student.*

What is an owl's favorite mystery?

A whooo-dunit.

How did the owl with laryngitis feel?

He didn't give a hoot.

What does an educated owl say?

Whom.

PARROTS AND PARAKEETS

What did the parrot say on
Independence Day?

"Polly wanna firecracker."

What did the starving parrot say?

> *"Polly wanna cheeseburger!"*

What do you get when you cross a parrot with a whippoorwill?

> *A bird that can sing both the words and the music.*

Bonnie: "Our parakeet bit my finger again this morning."

Benny: "Did you have to put anything on it?"

Bonnie: "Oh no. He likes it plain."

What do you call the Marines' pet bird?

A parrot trooper.

What do you say to a 200-pound parrot?
    "Here's your box of crackers. What else would you like?"

Steve: "How did your parakeet die?"
    Fred: "Flu."
    Steve: "Don't be silly. Parakeets don't die from the flu."
    Fred: "Mine did. He flew under a bus."

PEACOCKS

Have you heard the story about the peacock that crossed the road?

It really is a colorful tail. . . .

PENGUINS

What do you call a penguin in the desert?

Lost.

PIGS

Why shouldn't you tell a pig a secret?

Because he's a squealer.

PLATYPUSES

What's the favorite sport of platypuses?

Bill-iards.

PORCUPINES

Why do porcupines never lose games?

Because they always have more points than any other animal.

What did the boy porcupine say after he kissed the girl porcupine?

"Ouch!"

PRAIRIE DOGS

What goes 80 miles an hour underground?

A prairie dog on a motorcycle.

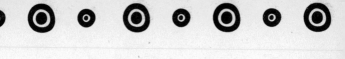

PRAYING MANTISES

Why do praying mantises have antennae?

*Cable service isn't available
yet in their neighborhood.*

RABBITS

**What do you call a rabbit with the
sniffles?**

A runny bunny.

How do you catch a rabbit?

*Hide in the bushes and
sound like a carrot.*

Where do injured rabbits go?

To the hopspital.

How do you catch a unique rabbit?

Unique up on it.

How do you catch a tame rabbit?

Tame way. Unique up on it.

What did the pink rabbit say to the blue rabbit?

"Cheer up!"

RATS

What does a 30-pound rat say?

"Here, kitty-kitty. . . ."

What do you call a dozen rats?

Scary.

What do rats keep in the glove compartments of their cars?

Rodent maps.

SHARKS

What is a shark's favorite game?

Swallow the leader.

Swimmer: "Are you sure there aren't any sharks along this beach?"

Lifeguard: "Oh yes, I'm sure. They don't get along well with the alligators."

SHEEP

A flock of lambs was playing in the meadow. "Baa! Baa! Baa!" they called merrily—except one lamb, who insisted, "Moo! Moo! Moo!"

"What are you saying?" they demanded.
"I'm practicing a foreign language."

Where do sheep go on vacation?

To the Baahaamaas.

Where do sheep get their hair cut?

At the baa-ber shop.

How do sheep stay warm?

With their central bleating system.

SKUNKS

"Look over there!" said the frightened skunk to his pal. "There's a human with a gun, and he's getting closer and closer! What are we going to do?"

The second skunk bowed his head and calmly replied, "Let us spray."

"Do you think the skunk would be considered a very popular animal?" the teacher asked.

"Not exactly—but it's always the scenter of attention," the student answered.

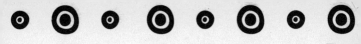

Why do skunks smell so bad?

Cheap cologne.

What's black and white and furry and moves on sixteen wheels?

A skunk on skates.

How do you make a skunk stop smelling?

Pinch its nose.

How many skunks does it take to smell up a neighborhood?

Just a phew.

Did you hear about the skunk that went to church?

He had his own pew.

SNAiLS

How do snails get across oceans?

In snailboats.

What did the snail say when he hitched a ride on the turtle?

"Wheeeee!"

SNAKES

What do you call a snake who gets elected mayor?

A civil serpent.

Why did the zoo veterinarian refuse to wear a necktie?

She already had a boa-tie.

What did Shane say when his pet snake crawled into the garbage disposal?

"It won't be long now."

Why is a snake so smart?

Because you can't pull its leg.

What kind of snake is good at math?

An adder.

SPIDERS

Where do spiders turn when they need to know how to spell a word?

To Web-ster's Dictionary.

How do spiders prefer their corn?

On the cobweb.

Why do spiders spin webs?

No one's ever taught them to crochet.

How do you find a spider on the Internet?

Check out his website.

SQUIRRELS

What kind of flowers would you give an absentminded squirrel?

Forget-me-nuts.

SWANS

Brother: "It's a good thing you're not a swan."
Sister: "Why?"
Brother: "You can't swim and you can't fly."

TICKS

What kind of insects live on the moon?

Lunarticks.

TIGERS

Teacher: "Jerry, name an animal that's a carnivore."

Jerry: "A tiger."

Teacher: "That's good. Beryl, can you name a carnivore?"

Beryl: "Another tiger."

TURTLES

What was the turtle doing on the Los Angeles freeway?

Record time.

Ingrid had caught a pond turtle and kept it in captivity for a couple of days, until her parents convinced her the little animal would be much happier in the wild. Her mother was very pleased when she saw Ingrid carrying the turtle out the back door.

"Where are you taking it?" her mother asked.

"Back to the pond."

"That's wonderful, honey!"

But the next day, Ingrid's mother noticed the turtle was still around. She saw Ingrid walking out the front door with it in her palm.

"I thought you set the turtle free yesterday," her mother said.

"No, I just took it back to the pond for a visit. Today I'm taking it to the beach."

Turtle to turtle: "Don't you just love the sound of rain on your roof?"

Why did the shy turtle force himself to go to the dance?

He wanted to come out of his shell.

A turtle is mugged by three snails, but when the police ask the turtle to give a description of what happened, all he can say is, "I don't know, Officer. It all happened so fast!"

WASPS

Where do you treat an injured wasp?

At the waspital.

What country do wasps come from?

Stingapore.

WOODPECKERS

What goes "peck-peck-peck-peck" and usually points to the north?

A magnetic woodpecker.

What is a woodpecker's favorite kind of joke?

A knock-knock.

WORMS

Where do worms prefer to shop?

In the Big Apple.

ZEBRAS

What's black and white and has a red nose?

> *Rudolph the red-nosed zebra.*

DIFFERENT ANIMALS TOGETHER

What do you get when you cross a tiger and a gnat?

> *A man-eating gnat.*

A pair of zebras were wandering in Africa when they heard the thunderous sound of hooves over the horizon. A massive herd of giraffes appeared, running their way in a blinding cloud of dust. The zebras took cover behind a tree and waited for the giraffes to pass. Then they continued wandering.

A few hours later, another large herd of giraffes approached, stirring up a storm of dust. Again, the zebras got out of the way.

Near sundown, they found themselves in the path of a third mob of giraffes. Standing behind a rock, coughing from the thick dust as the tall animals rushed past, one zebra turned to the other and said, "I think we should move away. There's too much giraffic around here to suit me."

"Oh no! The weather forecaster is calling for rain!" the kangaroo groaned to the rabbit.

"What's the problem with that?" asked the rabbit. "We could use some rain."

"Yes, but that means my children will have to stay inside to play."

"I love my pets," said Natasha. "It takes me five minutes just to say good-bye to them each morning before I come to school."

"What kind of pets do you have?" asked Mike.

"Three kittens, a hamster, and two dogs."

"Well, I certainly understand. It takes me more than an hour to say good-bye to my pets every morning."

"What kind of pets do you have?"

"I have fourteen goldfish and an ant farm."

Mike: "I heard you got kicked out of the zoo last week."

Ike: "Yeah, for feeding the squirrels."

Mike: "Wow, I know they don't like for people to feed the animals, but that seems like strong punishment."

Ike: "Actually, I was feeding the squirrels to the cougars."

What keys are found in the animal kingdom?

Donkeys, monkeys, and turkeys.

What do you get when you cross a polar bear and a sloth?

> *A giant, white, furry animal that sleeps while hanging upside-down from icicles.*

Amanda went to the pet store and told the clerk, "I want a *big* bag of bird seed."

"You must be planning to feed a lot of sparrows," said the clerk.

"No, actually, I'm planning to dye the seed blue and plant a *big* crop of bluebirds."

SECTION 2

SCHOOL AND ITS SUNDRY SUBJECTS

*A wise man will hear,
and will increase learning.*

PROVERBS 1:5

◎ • ◎ • ◎ • ◎

Okay, maybe school isn't always fun. . .but it is important. You probly don't understand it now, but trust us: Chances are you won't make a living playing Xbox. (If you can find the misspelling in the previous sentence, maybe you'll be a proofreader someday. . . in the meantime, enjoy some school-related jokes!)

SCHOOL iN GENERAL

When little Josie came home from her first day at school, her mother asked, "So how do you like school, Josie?"

"Closed," Josie said.

Nina came home from school and told her mother, "Our teachers talk to themselves too much."

"Really? Do you think they realize it?"

"Nah. They think students are listening to them."

Teacher: "How can one child make so many mistakes in one day?"

Student: "By getting up early."

"What did you score on those two exams today?" Gina's mother asked as Gina wearily flung her backpack on the dining table.

"A hundred," Gina replied.

"That's wonderful! You've never made an A in history before!"

"Well, actually, I scored fifty in history and fifty in math."

"Mindy, why are your grades so low on this report card?" Mother asked.

"Oh, it's that time of year," Mindy said. "You know everything is marked down after the holiday season."

Linda: "The teacher caught Winkie cheating on his reading test."

Rob: "Winkie knows cheating is dishonest. That was silly."

Linda: "Yeah—and even worse than you think."

Rob: "What do you mean?"

Linda: "The way the teacher knew he had cheated was his answer to the fourth question. The student sitting in front of him wrote, 'I don't know the answer.' Winkie wrote, 'I don't know the answer, either.'"

Two children met for the first time while walking home at the end of the first day of school.

"What's your name?" asked one.

"Jim White. What's yours?"

"Pete."

"Got a last name?"

"Well, I used to think my name was Pete Jenkins. But after today, I think it's Pete Be-quiet."

"I have good news and bad news," said the teacher. "The good news is that we're having only half a day of school this morning."

The class went wild with joy until the teacher quieted them.

"The bad news," he said, "is that we'll have the other half this afternoon."

"Did you play hooky from school yesterday to go fishing?" the teacher asked.

"No, sir," said Dennis. "I played hooky to go to the carnival."

"I didn't see you in any of our classes yesterday," said Kimberly. "You must've missed school."

"Not much," said Kenneth.

"Did you learn anything at school today?" Jeff's dad asked.

"I guess not," Jeff said. "They're making us return tomorrow."

Mother was reading in the den when Beth came to the door. "Mom, do you think you could sign your name in the dark?"

"I've never tried, dear, but I probably could."

"Good!" said Beth, switching off the light. "I need for you to sign my report card."

Mother was eager to hear about Brenda's first day at school. "So how do you think you're doing so far?"

"Well, apparently, I'm one of the advanced students," Brenda remarked.

"Oh, really? What makes you think that?"

"They put me at the head of a row."

A little boy walked up to the teacher's desk and said, "Miss Phillips, I've got bad news for you."

"What is it?" asked Miss Phillips.

"I'm afraid you're in big trouble."

"And why is that?"

"Well, my father says if my grades don't pick up, somebody's in big trouble."

Teacher: "You didn't answer the last two questions on the test."

Student: "Oh. Well, the answers are stuck inside my pen."

Why did Jerome go to night school?

So he could learn to read in the dark.

Teacher: "Why haven't you turned in your homework?"

Student: "I accidentally used the paper to make a paper airplane."

Teacher: "Where's the airplane?"

Student: "Somebody skyjacked it."

Perry: "Your lunch box has a glass top. That's neat!"

    Tammy: "Yes. When I'm on the bus, I can easily tell whether I'm going to school or going home."

Teacher: "Are you having trouble with the test questions?"

    Student: "Just with the answers."

A student drew a picture of a stagecoach with no wheels.

    "What holds it up?" asked the teacher. "Outlaws."

Wally: "I heard you had to stay in at recess. Did the teacher make you write the same sentence over and over?"

Henry: "No. She kept me busy, though."

Wally: "Doing what?"

Henry: "She gave me a piece of paper that said 'See other side.' "

Wally: "So what did it say on the other side?"

Henry: "That side said 'See other side,' too."

Mother: "What did you learn in school today?"

Elena: "We learned to say, 'Yes, ma'am' and 'Yes, sir.' "

Mother: "That's wonderful! You'll remember it, won't you?"

Elena: "Yeah, I guess."

When do leaves start to turn?

The night before a big test.

What's the favorite drink of cheerleaders?

Root beer.

ABC'S

Teacher: "What are zebras good for?"

Student: "To illustrate the letter 'z.' "

Teacher: "Shirley, compose a sentence that begins with 'I.'"

Shirley: "I is—"

Teacher: "Never say, 'I is.' It's 'He is' or 'She is,' but 'I am.' Begin your sentence, 'I am....'"

Shirley: "I am the ninth letter of the alphabet."

Why was Mrs. Johnson's class abuzz?

It was having a spelling bee.

First-grade teacher: "Hubie, what comes after 'g'?"

Hubie: "Whiz."

ARITHMETIC

"If you have ten pieces of bubble gum and you give away four, what do you have then?" the teacher asked.

"I have six pieces of gum and four new friends!" the student figured.

Teacher: "Two trains are headed toward each other on the same track. They're both traveling sixty miles per hour, and they're thirty miles apart. How soon will they collide?"

Student: "Much too soon."

Where do numbers take a bath?

In mathtubs.

"My math teacher doesn't make sense," said Janet.

"Why do you think that?" asked Shayna.

"Yesterday she taught us that nine plus one equals ten. Today she claims seven plus three equals ten."

Teacher: "Richie, if I offered you a choice between a basket with 36 bananas and a basket with 63 bananas, which would you choose?"

Richie: "The basket with 36 bananas."

Teacher: "Now Richie, surely you know 63 is more than 36."

Richie: "Yes, ma'am. That's why I'd pick the first basket. I can't stand bananas."

Teacher: "How many seconds in a minute?"

Don: "Sixty."

Teacher: "That's right. So how many seconds in an hour?"

Don, after a long calculation: "Three thousand, six hundred."

Teacher: "Very good! Now, this is a hard one: How many seconds in a year?"

Don: "Twelve."

Teacher: "Twelve? How do you get that?"

Don: "January 2nd, February 2nd, March 2nd..."

Teacher: "If you found a dollar in your left trousers pocket and 65 cents in your right pocket, what would you have?"

Student: "Somebody else's britches."

ART

Art teacher: "I asked you to draw a cow eating some grass, but you've only drawn the cow."

Student: "The cow ate all the grass!"

Art teacher: "I asked that you draw a horse and wagon. Why did you only draw a horse?"

Student: "I thought the horse would draw the wagon."

A second-grade teacher asked her students to draw examples of rings. She slowly walked around the room, noting their ideas. At Ed's desk, she stopped suddenly.

"Ed," she said, "those are all squares and rectangles."

"No they aren't," replied Ed. "They're boxing rings."

Belle: "The art teacher doesn't like what I'm making."

Dad: "Why is that—what are you making?"

Belle: "Mistakes."

Yvonne's parents received a note from her second-grade teacher.

"Yvonne is a wonderful student," the teacher wrote, "but when we have art and coloring projects, she draws everything in dark blue. Grass, flowers, people, the sky, houses, cars, trees—everything is dark blue. This is unusual for a second-grade student. Might there be an explanation? If there is some sort of emotional problem, I would like to work with you to resolve it as quickly as possible."

That night, Yvonne's parents sat down with her and asked her why everything she drew was in dark blue. "Why is that such a special color to you?" they asked her.

"Well," she began slowly, "I didn't want to tell you, but a couple of weeks ago I lost my box of crayons. The only one I have left is the dark blue one I found in the bottom of my backpack...."

BIOLOGY

Teacher: "Resa, name five animals you might find in Africa."

Resa: "A lion, an elephant. . .and three zebras."

Teacher: "What family does the octopus belong to?"

Student: "Nobody's that I know."

Teacher: "Where are elephants found?"

Student: "I don't know. They're so big I didn't think they could get lost!"

Teacher: "Do we get fur from a grizzly bear?"
   Student: "I'd get as fur from him as possible!"

COMPUTER CLASS

How did the computer student get out of class?

He pressed the ESCAPE key.

What is the favorite snack of computer students?

Chips.

What did the computer students have for a little snack?

Microchips.

Why did the computer student get up and leave the classroom?

To go have a byte of lunch.

Teacher: "Who was the first American president to use a computer?"
Student: "Warren G. Hard Drive."

Why did the school's computer die?

It had a terminal illness.

How are computers like soldiers?

They all have to boot up.

ENGLISH

"What is a synonym?" the English teacher asked.

"It's one of the words I use when I can't spell the main word," the honest student replied.

Teacher: "Have you ever read much Shakespeare before now?"

New student: "I don't think so. Who wrote it?"

Teacher: "Jory, what do you think of Shakespeare's writings?"

Jory: "I think much of what he wrote was a dreadful tragedy."

GEOGRAPHY

Teacher: "Do you think it was just as easy to explore the Arctic as it was Antarctica?"

Student: "I don't know. . . .There's a world of difference."

What's the capital of Wyoming?

That's easy: "W."

Marcie: "How do you spell 'inneapolis'?"

Slater: "Don't you mean 'Minneapolis'?"

Marcie: "No, I've already got the 'M.'"

The teacher asked Marie, "Please go to the map and locate Cuba."

Marie quickly found Cuba on the map at the front of the room.

"That's good, Marie. Now class, can anyone tell me who discovered Cuba?"

Derek quickly raised his hand. "Marie!"

GOVERNMENT

Teacher: "Who's the Speaker of the House?"
Student: "Daddy."

Where have English kings and queens always been crowned?

On the head.

Where did Lincoln sign the Emancipation Proclamation?

At the bottom of the last page.

HISTORY

Teacher: "Who was the first brother to fly an airplane at Kitty Hawk, North Carolina? Was it Orville or Wilbur?"

"Orville!" shouted one student.

"Wilbur!" shouted another.

"They're both Wright," said a third.

Why were the Wright Brothers first in flight?

Because they weren't wrong.

"What can you tell us about the Iron Age?" asked the teacher.

The student thought a moment. "Well, I imagine things got pretty rusty after heavy rains."

How did medieval soldiers learn to fight?

They enrolled in knight classes.

History teacher: "Why were the Middle Ages called the 'Dark Ages'?"

Student: "Because of all the knights."

Why did Columbus sail to America?

It was faster than swimming.

Teacher: "How long did the Hundred Years' War last?"

Student: "I don't know. Ten years?"

Teacher: "No! Think carefully. How old is a five-year-old horse?"

Student, thoughtfully: "Oh, five years old!"

Teacher: "That's right. So how long did the Hundred Years' War last?"

Student: "Now I get it—five years!"

Teacher: "What is Abraham Lincoln most famous for?"

Student: "The $5 bill."

Teacher: "What was the Romans' most famous achievement?"

Student: "They could read Latin."

History teacher: "Now Wally, what can you tell us about President Millard Fillmore?"

Wally: "He's dead."

Baker: "I wish I'd been born about four thousand years ago."

Brewster: "Why?"

Baker: "So I wouldn't have to learn so much history."

How did the ancient Vikings communicate?

Norse Code.

What do history teachers talk about when they get together?

The old days.

Teacher: "In the Old West, what was cowhide mainly used for?"

Student: "To keep the cow in one piece?"

MUSIC

"Which musicians are usually the meanest?" Danielle asked.

"It's a toss-up," guessed Ellen, "between the ones who beat the drums and the ones who pick on the guitars."

Which composer is squirrels' all-time favorite?

Tchaikovsky. He wrote "The Nutcracker."

What kind of snake has red and yellow bands, is highly dangerous, and sings tenor?

A choral snake.

"How was the symphony concert?"

"It was wonderful! The orchestra played Vivaldi."

"Who won?"

"Can you carry a tune at all?" the play director asked the final tryout after a long day of auditions.

"I'll let you judge that for yourself." The student confidently launched into a terrible, loud rendition of a well-known popular song.

"Well, what do you think? Can I carry a tune?"

"Yes," said the teacher. "Please carry it out and close the door behind you."

What do a piano and a newspaper reporter have in common?

They both make notes.

"May I have the pleasure of the next dance?" Mr. Mozart asked Mrs. Mozart.

"Wait just one minuet," said Mrs. Mozart.

"Mark, I just found your guitar outside in the garbage can!" his mother said.

"I know. I put it there."

"That was your birthday present! You waited months to get it."

"Yeah, but it's no good. There's a big round hole in the middle of the sound box."

Adam: "I crossed a dog with a piano student."

    Vera: "What did you get?"

    Adam: "A dog whose bark was worse than her bite."

Claire: "Those are cute bongos you have for earrings. They're so tiny! Can you really play them?"

    Brittany: "Yes. Those are my ear drums."

Sheila: "Why does Francis Scott Key get credit for 'The Star-Spangled Banner'?"

    Richie: "I guess because he learned all the words before anyone else."

What did the pianist do after his wrists developed carpal tunnel syndrome?

Played by ear.

What brass instrument is twice as large as a tuba?

A fourba.

Erskine: "I think I need to clean my tuba."

Band director: "Try this tuba toothpaste."

"I know a woman who can sing alto and soprano at the same time."
   "How does she do that?"
   "She has two heads."

Patrice: "What's a hobo?"
   Nicole: "I think it's a wind instrument."

Meredith: "I've been playing the piano for five years now."
   Ethan: "Do you ever stop to go to the bathroom?"

What's a geologist's favorite kind of music?

Rock.

Why was the lemon banned from the orchestra?

It hit too many sour notes.

How do you keep your arm from going to sleep?

Wear a singing wristwatch.

Patient: "I've swallowed my harmonica."

Doctor: "Good thing you don't play the guitar."

Clive: "It sure was an interesting symphony concert last night. The tuba player's wig slid off into the bell of his horn!"

Harry: "Oh no! Did they stop the concert?"

Clive: "No. He just blew his top and went right on playing."

Steven: "I wish you sang only Christmas carols."

  Mickey: "Why?"

  Steven: "Then I'd only have to listen to you one month out of the year."

SCIENCE

Where do stars and planets go to school?

At the universe-ity.

"I didn't understand the science teacher's lesson about the sky today," said Jan.

  "Why not?" asked her father.

  "It was way over my head."

What do you call four-day-old pizza?

A science project.

Teacher: "Can you name something that's harder than a diamond?"

Student: "Yes—paying for one."

"The spaceships of the next century will travel faster than the speed of light!" the science teacher marveled to her class.

"Then what kind of lights will they have inside them?" asked a student.

Teacher: "What do you call a star with a tail?"
    Student: "Mickey Mouse!"

After a lesson in the weather in the month of March, the teacher asked her class, "What is it that comes in like a lion and goes out like a lamb?"
    A student answered, "My dad."

Teacher: "What can we do to stop polluting our waters?"
    Student: "Stop taking baths."

SOCIAL STUDIES

Teacher: What language do they speak in Cuba?
    Franky: "Cubic."

Teacher: "Which is farther away, Australia or the moon?"
    Dave: "Australia. You can see the moon at night."

"Who invented the bow and arrow?" asked the teacher.

"Cavemen!" Gary called out enthusiastically.

"Cavemen? And what do you suppose prompted cavemen to come up with the bow and arrow?"

"Uh. . .somebody kept stealing their wheel?"

SPELLING

Teacher: "Robert, how do you spell 'elevate'?"

Robert: "E-l-a-v-a-t."

Teacher: "No, that's not the way it's spelled in the dictionary."

Robert: "You asked me how I spelled it, not the dictionary."

"Gayle, your handwriting is terrible," her father said.

"Yes, I know. I scribble deliberately."

"Why don't you want to write clearly?"

"This way, it's harder for the teacher to catch all my misspellings."

"Trina, you seem to be having a lot of trouble with your spelling assignments," the teacher said.

"Yes. I guess words intimidate me."

"But they're only words! Words can't hurt you."

"I suppose not—unless you get hit by a dictionary."

Teacher: "Jamie, how do you spell 'canoe'?"
Jamie: "K-n-e-w."

VOCABULARY

"Vocabulary test tomorrow, rain or shine," reminded the teacher as the class was dismissed.

"What if it snows?" asked Will hopefully.

Teacher: "Kenny, compose a sentence using the word 'archaic.'"

Kenny: "We all know we can't have archaic and eat it, too."

SECTION 3

ROCK-ROCKS AND KNIDDLES. . . UH, KNOCK-KNOCKS AND RIDDLES, THAT IS

Son of man, put forth a riddle, and speak a parable unto the house of Israel. . . .

EZEKIEL 17:2

◉ ○ ◉ ○ ◉ ○ ◉

Seriously. . .there are riddles in the Bible? Yeah, a couple. But we have a whole bunch here. . .along with plenty of silly knock-knock jokes. Be ready to laugh, groan, or scratch your head in confusion. Then pass 'em on to a friend!

WHO'S THERE?

Knock-knock.
Who's there?
Eddie.
Eddie who?
Eddiebody who comes too close to me might catch my cold.

Knock-knock.
Who's there?
Maybe.
Maybe who?
Maybe-bee gun is empty. Please sell may some more bee-bees.

Knock-knock.

Who's there?

Shorty.

Shorty who?

Shorty Simmons, who can't reach the doorbell.

Knock-knock.

Who's there?

Pasture.

Pasture who?

Pasture bedtime. Go to sleep.

Knock-knock.

Who's there?

Annie.

Annie who?

Annie time you're ready, come out and play. We're waiting on you.

Knock-knock.
Who's there?
Europe.
Europe who?
Europe mighty early this morning.

Knock-knock.
Who's there?
Atch.
Atch who?
Sorry you have a cold.

Knock-knock.
Who's there?
Howie.
Howie who?
Howie gonna win the baseball game if you won't come out and play?

Knock-knock.
> Who's there?
> Butcher.
> Butcher who?
> Butcher hands up! This is a robbery!

Knock-knock.
> Who's there?
> Abbey.
> Abbey who?
> Abbey birthday to you...

Knock-knock.
> Who's there?
> Howard.
> Howard who?
> Howard is it to lift a piano?

Knock-knock.
>Who's there?
>Pasta.
>Pasta who?
>Pasta gravy, please.

Knock-knock.
>Who's there?
>Luke.
>Luke who?
>Luke at me twirl my hula-hoop!

Knock-knock.
>Who's there?
>Irish.
>Irish who?
>Irish you would open the door.

Knock-knock.
>Who's there?
>Peas.
>Peas who?
>Peas open the door and let me in.

Knock-knock.
>Who's there?
>Tock.
>Tock who?
>Tock to me. I'm lonely.

Knock-knock.
>Who's there?
>Midas.
>Midas who?
>Midas well let me in. I'm not going anywhere.

Knock-knock.

Who's there?

Phillip.

Phillip who?

Phillip the dog's water bowl, please. He's very thirsty.

Knock-knock.

Who's there?

Lena.

Lena who?

Lena little closer. I don't hear too good.

Knock-knock.

Who's there?

Fido.

Fido who?

Fido known you lived here, I'do come to visit sooner.

Knock-knock.
　　Who's there?
　　Juneau.
　　Juneau who?
　　Juneau I was your next-door neighbor?

Knock-knock.
　　Who's there?
　　Celeste.
　　Celeste who?
　　Celeste time I'll ever ask you to come out
and play.

Knock-knock.
　　Who's there?
　　Lettuce.
　　Lettuce who?
　　Lettuce in! It's raining out here!

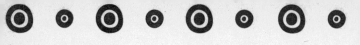

Knock-knock.
    Who's there?
    Sherwood.
    Sherwood who?
    Sherwood like to play with y'all this
afternoon.

Knock-knock.
    Who's there?
    Police.
    Police who?
    Police open the door.

Knock-knock.
    Who's there?
    Kenya.
    Kenya who?
    Kenya gimme a dollar to buy a pack of gum?

Knock-knock.
  Who's there?
  Dune.
  Dune who?
  Dune anything in particular this afternoon?

Knock-knock.
  Who's there?
  Jess.
  Jess who?
  Jess open the
door and don't ask
questions.

Knock-knock.
Who's there?
Anita.
Anita who?
Anita flashlight so I can see in the dark.

Knock-knock.
Who's there?
Stan.
Stan who?
Stan back. I'm coming in.

Knock-knock.
Who's there?
Max.
Max who?
Max me hungry just smellin' those hamburgers on the grill.

Q&A

What's the most successful thing government has ever invented?

The postage stamp, because it always sticks to its task until completion.

What always seems to be behind time?

A clock face.

What kind of ears do you find on a train engine?

Engineers.

What can you break just by calling its name?

Silence.

Jim was three years old on his last birthday and will be five years old on his next birthday. How can that be?

Today is his fourth birthday.

What never asks questions but gets a lot of answers?

A doorbell.

What word contains three *e*'s but only one letter?

"Envelope."

How do seven cousins divide five potatoes?

Mash them.

What are ten things in life you can always count on?

Your fingers.

What is cut and spread out on the table but never eaten?

A deck of cards.

What word in the English language is usually pronounced wrong even by scholars?

"Wrong."

What man shaves a dozen times a day?

A barber.

What button will you never lose?

Your belly button.

Why do skeletons stay home every night?

They have no body to go out with.

What's long, sharp, and one-eyed?

A needle.

Why were the ten toes nervous?

They were being followed by two heels.

What's the tiniest room you'll ever find?

A mushroom.

Which month has twenty-eight days?

All twelve of them.

What vegetable is a plumber's best friend?

A leek.

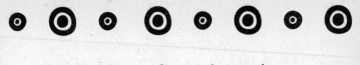

What gets larger if you take anything away from it?

A hole.

What has a fork and a mouth, but never eats food?

A river.

What did one math teacher say to the other?

I've got a problem.

Before the discovery of Australia, what was the earth's largest island?

Australia.

What's the noblest item ever made from a piece of wood?

A ruler.

SECTION 4

HI HO HI HO, IT'S OFF TO WORK THAT SOMEONE GOES

Six days shalt thou labour, and do all thy work. But the seventh day is the sabbath of the LORD thy God: in it thou shalt not do any work.

EXODUS 20:9–10

◉ ○ ◉ ○ ◉ ○ ◉

"Go clean your room!" "Feed the dog!" "Carry in these groceries!" Wow, it seems like a kid's work is never done. And grown-ups just aren't very sympathetic when you tell them you really *need* to finish a video game or TV show. We hope the following jokes will make everyone feel better.

BANKERS

Mike: "Did you hear Harry went to work at the bank?"

Ike: "No. Why does he want to work at a bank?"

Mike: "He heard there's money in it."

Husband: The bank returned your check.

Wife: Good, now I can use it for something else.

If money grew on trees, where would you keep it?

In a branch bank.

Two neighbor women were talking about their daughters. The first said, "My daughter is at the university. She's very bright, you know. Every time we get a letter from her, we have to go to the dictionary."

Her neighbor answered, "You are so fortunate. Every time we hear from our daughter, we have to go to the bank."

A spokesperson for the US Mint announced that a new fifty-cent piece was being issued to honor two great American patriots.

On one side of the coin would be Teddy Roosevelt and on the other side, Nathan Hale.

Asked why two people were going to be on the same coin, the spokesman replied, "Now when you toss a coin, you can simply call 'Ted's' or 'Hale's.' "

What has a head and a tail but no body?

A coin.

A big-city counterfeiter accidentally printed an eighteen-dollar bill. He decided the best place to unload the phony money would be in a small country town.

The counterfeiter selected a seemingly backwards village and entered the town's tiny bank. Handing the teller the bill, he asked, "Can I have change for this, please?"

The clerk pondered the $18 bill, then smiled and replied, "Sure, mister. Would you like two nines or three sixes?"

A man walked into a bank to hold it up and gave the teller a note that read, "This is a stickup. Give me all your money."

She passed a note back to him that said, "Fix your tie. We're taking your picture."

Why did the football coach go to the bank?

To get the quarter back.

"The prosecutor says she can produce five witnesses who saw you running from the bank with the money bags," the defense lawyer told his client.

"Oh, that's nothing," said the suspect. "I can produce two hundred witnesses who didn't see me running from the bank."

COOKS

Mother: "Valerie, why are you staring at that frozen orange juice container?"

Valerie: "Because it says *concentrate*."

"Oh no, not fried chicken," moaned little Cindy, coming into the kitchen for dinner. "I don't think I can stand to eat fried chicken this evening!"

"Why not?" asked her mother. "You liked it last night and the night before that, and the night before that...."

What's a miner's favorite food?

Coal slaw.

What did one strawberry say to the other?

"You sure got us into a jam this time."

"My Mom sure gets mean when she's in the kitchen," Scot said.

"What does she do?" asked Branden.

"She does things like beat the cake mix, mash the potatoes, whip the cream...."

What kind of cheese makes the best building material?

Cottage cheese.

What did the strawberry do when it couldn't get a date for the breakfast dance?

It invited a raisin.

What can you always find to eat if you're shipwrecked on a deserted island?

Lots of sand-wiches.

What's the difference between a moldy vegetable and a depressing song?

> One is a bad salad, and the other is a sad ballad.

Where do hot dogs dance?

> At meatballs.

How do you repair a broken casserole dish?

> With tomato paste.

What are the four seasons?

> Salt, pepper, Ketchup, and mayonnaise.

Mom, entering the kitchen: "I see you've been making chocolate chip cookies."

Marsha: "Can you smell them in the oven already?"

Mom: "No, but I notice M&M shells all over the floor."

DOCTORS

What did the doctor say to the woman who swallowed a spoon?

"Sit still and don't stir."

What do you call a bone specialist from Egypt?

A Cairopractor.

Woman: "My husband snores so loudly he keeps everybody in the house awake. What can we do?"

Doctor: "Try turning him on his side, massaging his shoulders and neck, and stuffing a washcloth into his mouth."

What do you call foot X-rays?

Footographs.

What do you call a surgeon with eight arms?

A doctopus.

Patient: "Doc, can you make house calls?"

Doctor: "That depends. How sick is the house?"

Eye doctor: "You need a new pair of glasses."

Patient: "How do you know that? You haven't examined me yet."

Doctor: "Because you just came in through my office window."

A woman barged into a doctor's office and demanded attention. "I dreamed I ate a giant marshmallow!" she screamed.

"Control yourself," said the receptionist. "It was only a dream."

"No dream! When I woke up, my pillow was missing!"

"Doc, I need a prescription."

"For yourself?"

"No, it's for my fireplace."

"Your fireplace? What seems to be the trouble?"

"I think it has the flue."

What kind of people enjoy bad health?

Doctors.

How is a surgeon like a comedian?

They both keep you in stitches.

On the way to preschool, the doctor let his daughter look at his stethoscope. His little daughter picked it up and began playing with it. This thrilled the father as he thought, *Perhaps one day she will follow in my footsteps and become a doctor.*

But then he heard her as she spoke into the instrument: "Welcome to McDonald's. May I take your order?"

What did the elevator say to the doctor?

"I'm coming down with something."

Dental patient: "How much would you charge to pull that bad tooth of mine?"

Dentist: "Our regular rate for pulling teeth is $75."

Patient: "Well, how much would you charge to loosen it for me?"

Why did the window have to be taken to the doctor's office?

It was suffering from windowpanes.

Why did the stand-up comedian go see the doctor?

She had tired feet.

"Doctor, my ear won't stop ringing."

"Then answer it."

How can a surgeon tell whether a patient is a librarian or an electrician?

The heart, lungs, liver, kidneys and stomach of a librarian are all numbered. The insides of an electrician are color-coded.

"Well, I believe we've solved your little hearing problem with these hearing aids," the doctor said. "That will be $900."

The patient pretended not to hear and walked out the door.

"My neck hurts every time I turn my head," complained the patient. "What should I do?"

"Don't turn your head," recommended the doctor.

The doctor was trying to cheer Artie, who'd sprained his wrist. "When you get out of this sling," the doctor told him, "you'll feel better than ever. You'll be able to write, catch Frisbees, and bounce basketballs with the best of them."

Artie stopped crying and brightened up. "Wow!" he said. "I've never been able to bounce a basketball before!"

"How do you feel?" asked the doctor.

"Like a dog," moaned Katie.

"Well, sit," the doctor said. "Stay."

"Doc, there's something wrong with my soda crackers."

"What are the symptoms?"

"They feel crumby."

FARMERS

Why did the farmer put razor blades in the potato patch?

He wanted to grow potato chips.

"I understand your bull wins first prize at the state fair each year," a stranger said to Farmer Jackson.

"That's right," said the farmer.

"What do you figure that bull's worth?" asked the stranger.

"Depends."

"What do you mean?"

"Depends on whether you wanna buy him or tax me for him."

Farmer: "You know, the people in my little town are smarter than the people in your big city."

City feller: "How do you get that?"

Farmer: "We know where LA is, but you don't know where Podunk is."

Where does the farmer wash his livestock?

At the hogwash.

Why did the farmer cross the road?

To catch his chickens.

Elaine: "My uncle just bought a farm that's a mile long and an inch wide."

Penny: "What does he think he can grow on land like that?"

Elaine: "Spaghetti, I guess."

Betsy and Pat were roaming the meadows of their grandparents' farm when they encountered a dangerous-looking bull.

"Are you afraid?" asked Pat.

"Not me," said Betsy. "I'm a vegetarian."

One rooster said to another, "You don't want to mess with the new rooster in the yard. He's mean."

"How do you know?" asked the second rooster.

"He came from a hard-boiled egg."

What did the farmer say to the sheep?

"Hey, ewe!"

Why did the farmer spend the day stomping his field?

He wanted mashed potatoes.

What did the farmer say to the hayfield?

"I'm very sorry, but I have to mow now."

What did the farmer do at the chocolate factory?

Milk chocolates.

Farmer: "Why aren't we having eggs for breakfast this morning?"

Farmer's wife: "I think the chicken mislaid them."

What did the pea patch say to the corn patch?

"Stop stalking me!"

First farmer: "Did the tornado damage your barn last night?"

Second farmer: "Don't know. Haven't found it yet."

Why did the farmer raise his children in a barn?

He wanted them to grow up in a stable environment.

When do you hear the shout, "Ready. . . . Set. . . . Hoe"?

At the beginning of a race between two farmers.

Robby: "What would you do if a bull charged?"
    Toby: "I'd give him all the time he wanted to pay off the bill."

Why should you never tell a secret in a cornfield?

Because the stalks have ears.

What did the farmer do when he finally caught the stray pig?

Put it in hamcuffs.

Why was the farmer so stressed out?

He was studying for the soil test.

"Daddy, what will we do with the hog after we butcher it?" asked the farm lad.

"Then we cure the meat."

The boy scratched his head. "Don't we have things backward, Daddy?"

"What do you mean, son?"

"Well, it seems to me that if we're gonna try to cure it, we should do that while the hog's still alive."

Farmer Brown and Farmer Jones were sitting in front of the country store listening to the birds in the distance.

"There's an old owl," said Farmer Brown. "Can you hear it call, 'Hoo, hoo'?"

"That's not an owl," said Farmer Jones. "It's a dove. It's saying, 'Coo, coo.'"

Farmer Brown shook his head sadly. "I'm ashamed to say I know you. You don't recognize a 'hoo' from a 'coo.'"

"What's the name of your hog?"

"Ballpoint."

"Why do you call it Ballpoint?"

"Actually, that's just its pen name."

"My dad grows corn so big he gets three dollars an ear at market," said one farm lad.

"That's nothing," said his friend. "My dad grows cantaloupe so big it takes only three to make a dozen."

What happened when the pigpen broke?

> *The pig had to start using a pencil.*

What did the farmer say when he found a hole in one of his pumpkins?

> *"I think I need a pumpkin patch."*

"How have you been doing?" asked Farmer Smith.

"Not too well," said Farmer Brown. "I just got out of the hospital."

"Land sakes! What was wrong?"

"I was kicked in the head by my old mule."

"What a terrible accident!"

"Wasn't an accident. I reckon the mule did it on purpose."

"My farmer cousin just got back from vacation. It was the first time he'd taken a break from farming in more than ten years."

"Where did he go?"

"To the beach."

"Oh, he must have enjoyed that!"

"He sure did. He was a little disappointed with surfing, though. The tractor engine kept dying out in the water."

What's the difference between a granary and a grandpa?

One's a corn bin. The other's your born kin.

Why did the farmer receive an award?

Because he was outstanding in his field.

SAILORS

The Cantrell family was vacationing aboard a Mississippi River steamboat.

"Is it true," little brother asked the steamboat captain, "that you know every stump and snag on the whole Mississippi River?"

"I sure do," the captain boasted.

Just then the boat ran up on a snag and stopped abruptly.

"There's one," the captain said.

What's a sailor's favorite deli item?

A submarine sandwich.

Who was the greatest chef in the British Navy?

Captain Cook.

What happens when you tell the ocean good-bye?

It waves.

How do they harvest the ocean floor?

With a subtractor.

What ocean animal is the most difficult to get along with?

The crab.

Who cleans house for fish and other sea creatures?

Mermaids.

Does an octopus go around all day shaking its legs or waving its arms?

What ocean always gets things absolutely right?

The Specific Ocean.

Albert: "Do you know what happens when you throw a gray rock into the Red Sea?"

Lon: "It changes color?"

Albert: "No, it gets wet."

What was Moby Dick's favorite dinner?

Fish and ships.

The new sailor was assigned to submarines, his dream since he was a young boy. He was trying to impress the master chief with his expertise learned in sub school.

The master chief cut him off quickly and said, "Listen, it's really simple. Add the number of times we dive to the number of times we surface. Divide that number by two. If the result isn't an even number, don't open the hatch."

⦿ ∘ ⦿ ∘ ⦿ ∘ ⦿

ODD JOBS. . .AND PEOPLE

Ed: "I have a job in a watch factory."
 Ned: "Oh really? What do you do?"
 Ed: "I just stand around and make faces."

Why did the archaeologist go bankrupt?

Because his career was in ruins.

Employee: "I've worked here for over twenty years and have never asked for a raise."

Employer: "That's why you've worked here for twenty years."

How is business?

Tailor: "Oh, it's so-so."

Electrician: "It's fairly light."

Author: "All right."

Farmer: "It's growing."

Astronomer: "Looking up!"

Elevator operator: "Well, it has its ups and downs."

Trash collector: "It's picking up."

Wife: "You don't look well. What's the matter?"

Husband: "You know those intelligence tests we give our employees?"

Wife: "Yes."

Husband: "Well, I took one today. . .and it's a good thing I own the company."

A Texan on a plane was bragging about land he owned.

The man sitting next to him asked, "How much property do you have?"

"Three acres," answered the Texan.

"That doesn't sound like all that much," replied the man. "Where is this property located?"

"Oh," said the Texan, "downtown Dallas."

What did Noah say when he'd finished loading the ark?

> *"Now I've herded everything."*

Barber: "Your hair is getting thin."
Client: "Who wants fat hair?"

Why do bakers work so hard?

> *Because they need the dough.*

A man was interviewing for a job. "And remember," said the interviewer, "we are very keen about cleanliness. Did you wipe your shoes on the mat before entering?"

"Oh yes, sir," replied the man.

The interviewer narrowed his eyes and said, "We are also very keen about the truth. There is no mat."

A store manager overheard one of his salesmen talking to a customer. "No, sir," said the salesmen. "We haven't had any for a while, and it doesn't look like we'll be getting any soon."

The manager was horrified and immediately called the salesman over to him. "Don't you ever tell a customer we're out of anything! Now, what did he want?"

"Rain," answered the salesman.

Two barbershops were in red-hot competition. One put up a sign advertising cheap haircuts. His competitor put up one that read, WE REPAIR CHEAP HAIRCUTS.

During a training exercise, an army unit was late for afternoon inspection.

"Where are those camouflage trucks?" the irate colonel barked.

"They're here somewhere," replied the sergeant, "but we can't find 'em."

Do you know why electricians are some of the smartest people?

They always keep up with current events.

How did the scientist invent bug spray?

She started from scratch.

What did the astronaut think of the takeoff?

It was a blast.

The owner of a large factory decided to make a surprise visit and check up on his staff.

As he walked through the plant, he noticed a young man doing nothing but leaning against the wall. He walked up to the young man and said angrily, "How much do you make a week?"

"Three hundred bucks," replied the young man.

Taking out his wallet, the owner counted out three hundred dollars, shoved it into the young man's hands, and said, "Here is a week's pay—now get out and don't come back!"

Turning to one of the supervisors, he asked, "Just how long had that lazy kid been working here?"

"He doesn't work here," said the supervisor. "He was just delivering a pizza."

Boss: "You should have been here at 8:00 sharp!"

Employee: "Why, what happened?"

A blacksmith finished hammering a white-hot horseshoe and threw it down on the ground to cool.

Just then, a man walked in, spotted the horseshoe, and picked it up. He quickly dropped it, biting his tongue to keep from screaming.

"Pretty hot, huh?" asked the blacksmith.

"Nah," the man said with a grimace. "It just doesn't take me long to look over a horseshoe."

"I have just developed the most powerful acid compound known to mankind," a scientist told her colleagues. "There is only one problem."

"What's that?" asked one.

"I can't find a container for it," she replied.

Why did the doughnut maker retire?

He was fed up with the hole business.

Two gas company servicemen were checking meters in a suburban neighborhood. They parked their truck at the end of the alley and worked their way to the other end. At the last house, a woman watched out her kitchen window as the men checked her gas meter. When they were finished checking the meter, the older of the two challenged his younger coworker to a race back to the truck.

As they came running up to the truck, they realized a woman was huffing and puffing right behind them. They stopped and asked her what was wrong.

In between breaths, she explained, "When I saw the two of you check my meter, then take off running, I figured I'd better run, too!"

How did the carpenter break his teeth?

He chewed his nails.

A young man was a very slow worker and found it difficult to keep a job. After a visit to the employment office, he was offered work at the local zoo.

When he arrived for his first day, the zookeeper, aware of the young man's reputation, told him to take care of the tortoises.

Later, the zookeeper dropped by to check on the new employee and found him standing by an empty enclosure with the gate open. "Where are all the tortoises?" he demanded.

"I can't believe it," said the young man. "I just opened the door and *whoosh*, they were gone!"

A guy walked into a large company and handed the boss an application. The executive scanned the sheet and saw that the applicant had been fired from every job he had ever held.

A fast-food manager was reviewing a potential employee's application and noted that the boy had never worked in a restaurant before.

"For a guy with no experience," the manager said, "you are certainly requesting a high wage."

"Well, sir," the applicant replied, "the work is much more difficult when you don't know what you're doing."

"Your work history is awful," the boss said. "You've been terminated from every job."

"That's true," the applicant replied.

"Well," the boss answered, "there isn't much positive about that!"

"Sure there is," said the applicant. "I'm not a quitter!"

A construction foreman had ten very lazy men working for him, so one day he decided to trick them into doing some work for a change.

"I have a really easy job today for the laziest one among you," he announced. "Will the laziest man please raise his hand."

Nine hands shot up.

"Why didn't you put your hand up?" he asked the tenth man.

"It was too much trouble."

Herb had spent all afternoon interviewing for a new job. He began by filling out all the papers. The human resources manager then questioned him at length about his training and past work experience. Herb then was given a tour of the plant and was introduced to the people he would be working with.

Finally, he was taken to the general manager's office. The manager rose from his chair, shook his hand, and asked him to sit down.

"You seem to be very qualified," he said, "and we would like for you to come work for us. We offer a good insurance plan and other benefits. We will pay you six hundred dollars a week starting today, and in three months, we'll raise it to seven hundred dollars a week. When would you like to start?"

"In three months," Herb replied.

A man applied for a job at a construction firm.

"We take turns making the coffee," said the foreman. "Do you know how to make coffee?"

"I sure do," said the applicant.

"And can you drive a forklift?"

"Why? Just how big is the coffeemaker?"

SECTION 5

Faith Funnies

*And the next sabbath day
came almost the whole city
together to hear the word of God.*

ACTS 13:44

◉ ● ◉ ● ◉ ● ◉

Bring a bunch of people together and something
funny is bound to happen. . .especially at church.
Want proof? Read on. . . .

BIBLE JOKES

Alice: "Grandma, were you on Noah's ark?"
Grandma: "Oh no."
Alice: "Then how did you survive the flood?"

Did the worms enter Noah's ark in pairs?

No, in apples.

Who was the first tennis player in the Bible?

Joseph. He served in Pharaoh's court.

What kind of lights did Noah put on the ark?

Floodlights.

Sunday school teacher: "Nora, what does the Bible have to say about the Dead Sea?"

Nora: "Dead? I didn't even know it was ill!"

The Sunday school teacher asked her pupils to draw a picture of Joseph, Mary, and the Christ child fleeing from Herod. Margie drew an airplane with three faces looking out the windows.

"That's interesting," the teacher said. "Where are they going?"

"Egypt," Margie replied.

"By airplane?"

"Yes, Pontius the pilot is driving."

Was Noah the first one out of the ark?

No, he came forth out of the ark.

What did Noah do for a living?

He was an ark-itect.

Shelby: "Do you know at what point in history God created Eve?"
   Sandra: "Right after He created Adam."

Who was most sorry when the Prodigal Son returned home?

The fatted calf.

"Who was the fastest runner in history?" asked Shelley.
   "Adam," said Mackie. "The Bible says he was first in the human race."

SUNDAY SCHOOL SiLLiES

A Sunday school teacher asked her fifth-grade class which events in the life of Jesus impressed them the most and which happenings they liked the best. These were some of the responses:

"When Jesus raised Lazarus from the dead."

"When He raised the twelve-year-old girl to life."

"When He helped the apostles catch so many fish that their boat began to sink."

But Frank's response was, "I like the story about the big crowd that loafs and fishes."

The Sunday school teacher asked her class, "Who wants to go to heaven?"

Everyone held up their hand expect for one young boy.

"James, don't you want to go to heaven when you die?"

"Oh yes, when I die, but I thought you were getting a bunch to go now."

"I used to think that King David was a hero, but I don't think that anymore," declared Bobby after Sunday School.

"Why not, Bobby?" asked his mother.

"I found out today that he killed the Jolly Green Giant."

A father was teaching his son to admire the beauty in nature.

"Look, Will," he exclaimed, "isn't that a beautiful sunset that God painted?"

"It sure is, Dad," he agreed, "especially since God had to paint it with His left hand."

The father was bewildered. "What do you mean—His left hand?"

"Well," he said, "my Sunday school teacher said that Jesus is sitting on God's right hand."

The Sunday school teacher, trying to get a response from his class of eight-year-old boys, said, "Boys, can't you imagine Noah on that ark, spending a lot of time fishing?"

One boy replied, "I don't think he did. He only had two worms!"

Sunday school teacher: "Taylor, do you disobey your parents?"

Taylor: "No, sir."

Sunday school teacher: "Do you ever use mean words?"

Taylor: "No, sir."

Sunday school teacher: "You must do *something* wrong every once in a while!"

Taylor: "Well, I don't always tell the truth."

A Sunday school class was reviewing the lesson of Jonah. "What is it that we can learn from the story of Jonah and the whale?" asked the teacher.

One student replied, "People make whales sick!"

Sunday school teacher: "Gretchen, what can you tell me about Goliath?"

Gretchen: "Goliath was the man David rocked to sleep."

A teacher asked her kindergarten class, "Can a bear take his warm coat off?"

"No," they all answered.

"Why not?"

There was a long silence. Finally, a young boy spoke up: "Because only God knows where the buttons are."

Dustin listened attentively to the Sunday school lesson about the parable of the Prodigal Son.

"And what happened when the Prodigal Son returned home?" asked the teacher at the end of the lesson.

"His father went to meet him and hurt himself," replied Dustin.

"Hurt himself?" asked the teacher. "Where did you learn that?"

"From the Bible," answered Dustin. "It says his father ran to meet him and fell on his neck."

The Sunday school teacher was explaining the story of Elijah and the false prophets of Baal. She explained how Elijah built the altar, put wood on it, cut the steer in pieces, and laid them upon the altar. Then Elijah commanded the people of God to fill four barrels with water and pour it over the altar. He had them do this four times.

"Can anyone tell me why God would ask Elijah to pour water over the steer on the altar?" asked the teacher.

A little girl excitedly answered, "To make the gravy!"

Little boy's prayer: "Dear God, please take care of my mommy and daddy and sister and grandma and grandpa. And please, God, take care of Yourself, or else we're all sunk!"

At Sunday school, Mr. Duncan told his students that God created everything, including human beings. Freddy seemed especially intent when Mr. Duncan explained that Eve was created out of one of Adam's ribs.

Later in the week, his mother noticed him lying on the floor and asked, "Freddy, what is the matter?"

Freddy responded, "I have a pain in my side. I think I'm gonna have a wife."

A young boy walked into his Sunday school class late. His teacher knew that he was usually very prompt, so she asked, "Ryan, is something wrong?"

The boy replied, "No. I wanted to go fishing, but my dad told me that I needed to go to church."

The teacher was very impressed and asked Ryan if his dad had explained to him why it was more important to go to church than to go fishing.

Ryan answered, "Yes. Dad said he didn't have enough bait for both of us."

A little boy had just gotten home from Sunday school. While his mother was cooking lunch, he asked, "Is it true that before you're born you're just dust and after you die you go back to being dust?"

"Yes, son. Why do you ask?"

"Well, that's what my Sunday school teacher said today."

"Yes, she's right. Now go on and wash your hands. Lunch will be ready in a few minutes."

About ten minutes later, she called for him to come for lunch. As they were sitting down to eat, the little boy asked again about being dust before you're born and after you die. Once again the mother informed her son that it was true.

The little boy looked at her and said, "Then you'd better go to my room pretty quick, because something under my bed is either coming or going!"

A Sunday school class was learning John 3:16. One child recited it, "For God so loved the world that He gave His only begotten Son, that whosoever believeth in Him should not perish, but have ever-laughing life."

Toward the end of Sunday school one morning, a little boy asked the teacher, "Are there animals in heaven?"

"What kind of animals?" the teacher asked.

"Animals—like cows and bees," said the boy.

"Well, I'm not sure," answered the teacher, "but I don't think they'll be necessary in heaven."

"But then where will we get enough milk and honey for everybody?" he asked.

"Wasn't it good that the shepherds put on clean clothes before they went to see baby Jesus?" asked the little boy.

His mother questioned, "How do you know they did that?"

"Well," he replied, "in Sunday school we sang 'While Shepherds Washed Their Socks by Night.' "

A Sunday school teacher was trying to convey the message of the story of the Good Samaritan. Finally, she asked, "Betsy, suppose you passed an empty lot and saw a man in ragged clothes lying on the ground, badly beaten up, and covered with blood. What would you do?"

The young girl answered, "I think I would throw up."

Definitions given by children in a Sunday school class:

Conversion: "The point after a touchdown."

Fast days: "The days you have to eat in a hurry."

Epistle: "The wife of an apostle."

A Sunday school teacher was discussing the Ten Commandments with her five-year-olds. After explaining the commandment that teaches us to "honor thy father and thy mother," she asked, "Is there a commandment that teaches us how we should treat our brothers and sisters?"

One little boy quickly answered, "Thou shalt not kill."

At Christmastime, the Sunday school teacher asked her students to draw a picture of the nativity. The children all drew wonderful pictures, variations of the same basic scene—Mary and Joseph, baby Jesus in the manger, the animals, the shepherds, and the wise men.

The teacher was somewhat confused by little Katie's picture, though. "What is that large box in front of everyone with the lines coming out from the top?" she asked Katie.

"Oh," she answered, "that's their TV!"

A Sunday school teacher was reading a Bible story to her class: "The man named Lot was warned to take his wife and flee out of the city, but his wife looked back and turned to salt."

A little boy asked softly, "What happened to the flea?"

Rebecca went to her Sunday school teacher after class. She asked, "If the people of Israel were Israelites, and the people of Canaan were Canaanites, do we call the people from Paris parasites?"

Grandma: Were you a good girl at church today, Missy?

Missy: Yes, I was. When the nice man offered me a whole plate of money, I said, "No, thank you."

Sunday school teacher: Phil, who was the first woman?

Phil: I don't know.

Sunday school teacher: I'll give you a hint. It had something to do with an apple.

Phil: Oh, I know. . .Granny Smith!

A Sunday school teacher asked her little children, as they were on the way to the church service, "And why should we be quiet in church?"

A little girl replied, "Because people are sleeping."

Livin' out the Faith

A mother was preparing pancakes for her sons, Jack and Chris. The boys began to argue over who would get the first pancake. Their mother saw the opportunity for a moral lesson. "If Jesus were sitting here, He would say, 'Let my brother have the first pancake; I can wait.'"

Jack turned to his younger brother and said, "Chris, you be Jesus!"

A man was lying on the grass and looking up at the sky. As he watched the clouds drift by, he asked, "God, how long is a million years?"

God answered, "To me, a million years is as a minute."

The man asked, "God, how much is a million dollars?"

God answered, "To me, a million dollars is as a penny."

The man then asked, "God, can I have a penny?"

God answered, "In a minute."

A woman and her five-year-old son were headed to McDonald's. On the way, they passed a car accident.

As was their habit when seeing an accident, they prayed for whoever was involved.

After the mother prayed, she asked her son if he would, too. "Please, God," he prayed, "don't let those cars be blocking the entrance to McDonald's."

A minister was visiting the home of a family in his congregation. Their little son ran in, holding a mouse by the tail.

"Don't worry, Mom, it's dead," he reported. We chased him, then hit him until..."

Just then he caught sight of the minister. He lowered his voice and eyes and finished, "...until God called him home."

A nurse on the pediatric ward, before listening to the children's chests, would fit the stethoscope into their ears and let them listen to their own hearts. Their eyes would always light up with awe.

"Listen," she said to little four-year-old Seth. "Do you hear it? What do you suppose that is?"

He listened to the strange tap-tap-tapping deep in his chest. Then his eyes lit up, and he exclaimed, "Is that Jesus knocking?"

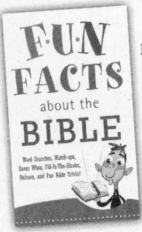